Dear Ex,

Love,
Lakeeya Natasha

TABLE OF CONTENTS

Dedication 1

How to read this book: 5

    Denial 7

    Bargaining 20

    Anger 44

    Depression 66

    Acceptance 100

bonus letters to my younger self, future self, and current self 163

How To Survive a Breakup 169

About the Author 171

Dedication

To my daughters, my son, my sissy, and my tribe- thank you for holding me down. When I couldn't find the strength to live, you breathed for me, you held me up until I could stand, and you were so patient with my grief. Thank you for seeing me and loving me unconditionally.

To my therapist- thank you for journeying with me in and out of the abyss. Thank you for seeing me and pushing me to see myself and re-imagine how I seen this heartbreak.

To my Lord and Savior, Jesus Christ- Thank you for always protecting me, guiding me, providing for me, and in my lowest moments reminding me of the Divine Plan on my Life found in Jeremiah 29:11 "For I know the plans I have for you", declares the Lord, "plans to prosper you and not harm you, plans to give you hope and a future."

I love you!

Dear Reader,

Just like any other loss, a breakup will take you through a journey through all the stages of grief. This book is a compilation of 100+ letters to my ex-husband that were never sent to him. He ghosted me and every time I tried to communicate with him, it only left me more frustrated and depressed. I wasn't given any answers or any closure. I started writing the letters for me then I quickly realized there are so many like me desiring closure they will never receive. I hope that this inspires, encourages, and validates each of you. Anyone that is in a healing journey because of the ending of a relationship- either from a relationship that the ending was well overdue or a relationship that you never thought would end, your feelings are valid. Your feelings are leading you down the path of your healing. Accept every emotion in this process. Nourish yourself with self-care, compassion, love, acceptance and forgiveness for allowing yourself to accept less than you deserved.

If ending a relationship with a narcissist, know that what happened to you was not your fault. Your only fault was to love someone more than you loved yourself yet as soon as you recognized your worthiness that recognition put the expiration date on your relationship. They needed you to stay broken, stay needing them, stay chasing their attention and affection. They needed you to stay chasing the version of them they presented in the love bombing phase (you know- that version of them that would move heaven and earth to be with you to stay with you). No matter how long you've been together as soon as you recognize who you are and that you are dealing with someone who thrives and profits off of using you, it will be difficult to stay, however, it may take some time to exit safely (physically, emotionally, and financially) so do not blame yourself or let anyone blame you for staying. So, I hope you are able to be released from this relationship intact, with wholeness, support, and protection. In some cases, the narcissist discards you, which you will one day find out was for the best and in other cases, you had to make a choice. Either way, this is painfully debilitating. I almost lost my mind and I am a mental health therapist. Narcissistic Abuse is a form of Domestic Violence and it does not discriminate so I stand with you and I speak for you.

It's completely normal to still feel the weight of a breakup, especially when there are unresolved feelings and hopes for reconciliation. However, it's important to remember that your value and worth are not tied to this relationship or its outcome. Healing takes time, and longing for the past is a natural part of that process. But this chapter is also an opportunity to rediscover yourself, your strength, and what you truly want and deserve. Take this time to focus on your own growth and happiness, knowing that you are whole on your own. You deserve someone who chooses you fully, and whether or not that happens with this person, the future holds new possibilities that can bring you joy and fulfillment. You are enough as you are, and your heart will find peace again.

There is a purpose behind your pain just like it was a purpose behind my pain if you can relate to any of my letters I see you. I feel you. I am you. Use this book as a way to journey through your own grief and know that we all will make it to the other side of this pain and find joy. Again, that is my wish for you. Thank you for supporting me in this healing journey. The first step for me was accepting that I was in a narcissistic abuse relationship but I did not know it was one until I left.

Sending you light and Love,

Keeya aka Queen

How to read this book:

The letters in this book were not written in any order. I wrote what I was feeling at the time and after I wrote each letter, I categorized them based on the stage of Grief it most represented. If you know anything about Grief, you know it is not linear. You can experience all 5 stages throughout one day or you can stay in one stage for years. The stages of grief, originally introduced by Elisabeth Kübler-Ross, are often associated with death and loss, but they can also apply to the end of significant relationships. A breakup can feel like the loss of a future you had envisioned, or a death of the person you were with, your ex-partner, so these stages often show up as part of the healing process. Each set of letters will have a brief description of the corresponding stage of change. It is not an all-inclusive summary or explanation (there are plenty free resources online for that) but enough for you to understand why I group the letters this way. I hope you feel seen in these letters or if this is not your experience, that this book will help you see others going through breakup sorrows in a new way. I hope this book inspires others to journal, write letters, or write a book because your pain matters, your story matters, and your healing definitely matters.

Trigger Warning Some of the letters will evoke negative thoughts and emotions, please take breaks, skip entries, use positive coping strategies, gain support from family/friends, and connect with a mental health professional if needed. I am a therapist, with my own therapist, yet during this time of my life and while writing this book, I had to increase my sessions to endure and overcome the emotional damage this relationship and subsequently breakup caused.

Denial

This stage involves disbelief and an inability to accept the relationship is over. It may feel like a bad dream you hope to wake up from. After a breakup, you might still cling to hope that things will work out, imagining that it's just a rough patch or a temporary separation. You may refrain from sharing the breakup news with friends and family because you don't want them to think differently of him/her when you reconnect.

Things I told myself:
"No, this can't be happening..."
"He doesn't know what he is doing"
"Just give him space, he will come back around"
"Maybe we just need a break to figure it out"
"He wouldn't do this to me, He wouldn't embarrass me like this"
"He would not have married me if he didn't want to be with me forever"

Lakeeya Natasha

Denial

Dear Ex,

Today I was at my family's house for a gender reveal for my little cousin and while there I pretended. I hate to have to pretend. I had to pretend to be happy. I was so happy for the young couple yet I had no happiness inside of me. It took all my strength but I pretended to be okay. PRETEND that we were still together when people asked. How are you, what you doing? They missed you, they wanted me to say hi to you. I smiled and said he's well, he's home. He's doing good. Thank you. I'll tell him. All along, I wish those words were true. I don't even know if you are okay. I don't even know where you were at that time. When I said it, I left. I hugged, I encouraged, I smiled, in all the while I couldn't wait to get into my car so I can stop pretending. I don't even know anymore whether I'm pretending for you or pretending for me. I cannot believe that you put me in this situation where I have to explain and you haven't even explained it to me. So I have to assume what your explanation is and share that.

How much should I share about my story? Just in case, you come around knowing you messed up. I know this is not possible because how would I ever trust you again? I'm always going to wait for the rug to be pulled from under me again. I would not be able to breathe or relax with you again. Yet, even still, I know I love you and I know I have to let you go. I can't pretend again.

Love,

Your once loyal wife.

Lakeeya Natasha

Dear Ex,

I can't believe you did this to me. I am so disappointed in you or who I thought you were. I don't even know what to trust anymore. It doesn't make sense. This wasn't supposed to happen.

- confused

Dear Ex,

I can't believe I am calling you my ex. I truly thought we were forever...

This is surreal. When people ask me about you or bring you up, I freeze. I don't want to

say what I know I should say: "We broke up"

It is like those words get stuck in my throat and I begin to choke on them. A knot in my chest develops and my stomach becomes nauseous. I get an instant headache. You literally make me sick. The thought of us not together makes me sick. And when I finally get up the nerve to tell someone the truth, their shocked reaction, my need to console them, my need to explain in the shortest amount of words so I don't break into tears and a million pieces makes me sick. I can't believe you did this to me.

-Sick & Broken-hearted

Dear Ex,

Am I dreaming this? I want to wake up from this nightmare.

-Sleep Walker

Dear Ex,

I am shocked to discover there was a thing called Covid Love. Covid allowed abusers and Narcissists to play. The last 4 years have been a whirlwind of highs and lows yet the highs weren't high enough to compare to how low you took me. Covid Love gets zero stars. I know how it happened but still don't know how it happened?

-Confused

Dear Ex,

Is it really over? So soon? I was preparing to spend my life with you. I wanted you to be the last person to touch my body, kiss my lips, and experience my WAP. I thought you wanted that too?

-Lost

Dear Ex,

I lied today. You know I hate to lie. I cringe every time someone mentions your name because I want to shout from the roof tops, "he is a piece of shit covered in glitter who is pretending to be gold". I don't know whether I lie for you or for me when someone asks about you. I can't believe the same people I was bragging about my great love to are the same people who I have to say it was nothing great about that love except for the level of damage it caused my psyche and my spirit. I can't believe I am still protective of you or am I protecting myself from the people who thought it was too good to be true?

What have you done to me?

Dear Ex,

I saw you today and I still feel sick to my stomach. You spoke to everyone except me at my daughter's party. Why come and if you felt obligated to come, why did you feel the need to stay? I did not shed a tear until I got home. I truly can't believe this is who you are. I still can't believe my friends and family talked to you like you are a normal person, like you didn't stomp on my heart. I have no words for anyone. I hate you for coming and for staying. I hate that you were laughing with people I thought were my friends. I just can't deal. I don't think I ever want to see you again but I know I will, at least for a little while longer. I can't believe this is my life now.

Dear Ex,

This can't be life. I didn't sign up for this.

Dear Ex,

Some days I forget I'm single. Some days I forget how I became single. Then a man comes along flirting and asking me if I have a man. When I say no, they look as shocked as I feel most days. Like, why? For a woman so ready to love, I stay alone or lonely.

Dear Ex,

I know what you did. I know what you said. I know what you made me do. Yet, I still can't believe it. I still can't believe how our relationship crashed and burned. I would not have bet my life if I thought you would ever hurt me this way. I bet my life that we would have been together forever. Maybe that's why I feel like I'm dying. I just can't believe it.

Bargaining

During this stage, you might think about what you could have done differently and might even attempt to reach out to your ex in hopes of reconciliation. You may offer to change, apologize excessively, or try to find a way to "fix" things, as part of the effort to undo the breakup. Replays of red flags you overlooked and small fights that didn't mean much in the moment gets amplified in your mind and all you can do is look for moments where you should of known this would have happened and make imaginary attempts to change the very real ending of your relationship. You ask yourself why you were not enough or what could have saved the relationship.

Things I told myself:
"Was I that bad to him?"
"Maybe I should not have said anything about his drinking"
"We shouldn't have gotten married, I guess he wasn't ready"

"I'll remind him why he chose me"
"We can go to therapy and fix this"

Bargaining

Dear Ex,

Woke up another day trying to make sense of all of this. This doesn't make sense to me.

Was our happiness real? Did you ever love me? Were there any signs or was I just dismissing the signs? I really cannot believe you've done this to me. I can't believe you could be so evil. The fact that you can go without talking to me. It's OK to not want to be with me like it's OK, I'm not everyone's cup of tea. I recognize that and I thought about what I could have done differently to keep you. And I recognized that anything I would have done, would of diminished who I was. I couldn't be anything but who I was with you and it's crazy because I never felt safe enough to be my true self with anyone else so I just knew this was forever.

I rallied the troops and designed your praises to let everyone know how great you are. Maybe that's why you needed me. Maybe because you were feeling so low so insecure. So low in your own esteem and in your brokenness, you needed someone like me to lift you up to make you more than who you were and I didn't see it.

DearEx,

I still don't know how you are. I met different versions of you in this past year. I felt I found my match but literally I found my manipulator. I partnered with my worse abuser. I never hurt as much as I hurt now. This is coming from a woman who at 3 years old was sexually assaulted. At 5 years old was consistently molested by my uncle. At 16, being raped. Only 19 and been cheated on by my husband who had a baby on me and became physically, emotionally, and financially abusive to me. My second husband was completely neglectful of my heart and used me for his financial stability. You knew all of this, appeared to accept me and demonized those people who hurt me. I overcame all those things just to land here? A 41-year-old woman broken yet again. I was never expecting to break by the hands of someone I gave my whole heart to. For the first time ever, I fully put my trust in another human being and this human being proceeded to dismantle me.

I'm disgusted, you disgust me.

You took something away from me. You took something I was willing to give to you freely. You took my heart. You took my trust. You took my loyalty. You took my commitment. For what?

And now you don't talk to me. You shut me out and then you can't explain to one person what I have done to you. A man with a big vocabulary using big fancy words now has nothing to say- you're ugly and evil. Some days I wake up hoping that this was all a dream and that I just let my anxiety get the best of me or I was just in a really deep sleep and I wake up next to you and you reassure me and you say no, I'm here. I love you. I would never hurt you. Didn't I show you that every day? But instead I wake up to this, never-ending nightmare. I know that it's over and I don't even know why.

Maybe I don't want to accept why because it was never meant to be. You knew that when you chose me that I was better than you. You knew that I was a better person than you. You resented me from day one. You resented the fact that you had to pretend to care about me. It was exhausting for you to pretend to be nice to so many people. To pretend to be my caregiver, my lover, my friend. How exhausted were you to pretend? Then you grew fatigued and let your mask slip and when you recognize that I could see you, you stop pretending and you created a war. You brought the war you had within you and turned it towards me. You made me the villain of your story instead of you taking ownership of your own shit, you made me question myself for months.

What could I have done differently to help you while you were diabolically setting up my demise, by making me feel crazy and causing me to be so stressed that I became sick then blame me for my sickness.

I can never not see you now. All I see is who you are. I wouldn't ever see you in that mask again. I hope all you can see is who I am. I hope you see me flourish. I hope you see me be loved correctly for real. I hope you recognize that you lost the one person that loved you for real. I was the one person that really wanted you to succeed. I hope you recognize you fumbled the wrong girl then you spend your life crying out to God. God is only one that can save you now. And when you talk to God, ask for forgiveness and not to ever be with me again because that ship has sailed, you will never kiss these lips again. You will never get between these thighs again. You will never have this woman to show off to the world how "good" you are as a man. But I do hope that you do find healing so no other woman has to go through what you put me through.

Sincerely,

Your Lesson

Lakeeya Natasha

Dear Ex,

I am trying not to get mad at myself every time I think of you. Please don't flatter yourself, I do not want you back. I'm still trying to figure out how did this happen. I understand you have no truth in you so you will never tell me the truth. You lack accountability so I will only frustrate myself asking you, why? Your lack of accountability is my closure. I would never want to be with someone that is that good of a liar. I guess my love for you makes me curious about, what makes some one become like you? A destroyer.

Curiously,

Your ex

Dear Ex,

Are you a boy having a midlife crisis or was our relationship your social experiment? Were you ever committed or was I always a game to you? Was I your shiny new toy that you discarded when you got bored or was it too tiresome to maintain the devoted man act? Were you trying out being a good person for few years or is this your cycle of narcissistic abuse?

-Survivor of you

Lakeeya Natasha

Dear Ex,

We made vows. We stood up in front of our friends and family professing our love for each other. Only 2 years later, to be announcing divorce. What a failure! Why did you even propose? The day you stole my engagement rings, was the day I knew it was over. I had hope that we would find

our way back during the separation but when you did that, I knew you already moved on. What was the point? I was in it for love. What were you in it for?

-Confused

Dear Ex,

You are a coward. You couldn't even tell me why you did what you did. Most people break up with a partner because one of five reasons- cheating, lying, stealing, disrespect, or withholding love or sex...I did none of these. What are you telling people I've done to you? What are you saying when people ask why are we not together? Did you tell them that one day you came into our room and said you not happy with YOUR life and then proceeded to dismantle OUR life?

Did you tell people that you have been pulling away since we said I Do but I didn't see it at first? Did you tell people that you gave me a vacuum cleaner from the flea market for Christmas? Did you tell them that you lied to our kids saying you would do what it takes to make our relationship work and keep our family intact? Did you tell everyone that you bought a red two door sports car and hid it from your wife? Did you tell them that you increased your drinking yet denied it every time your wife asked were you okay? Did you tell them that your wife suggested you go back to therapy for almost a year you're your reply was "my Mental health is the best it has ever been"? Did you tell them you stole your wife's engagement rings and when she asked about it you said you gave them back to your mom because they were heirlooms? Did you say you fired the marriage therapist after 2 sessions because she told you to stop calling your wife hostile? Did you tell everyone that you started a campaign in which your mother and daughter began calling me hostile yet neither of them can name one hostile thing I've done to you or them? Did you share that you stop complimenting your wife and treated her like she was invisible in public? Did you tell them that you were never turned down for sex? Did you tell them you are a pervert and all the nasty things you like to do yet you were never satisfied? Did you say that you have enough money to clear your wife's debt yet let her struggle to pay her bills? Did you tell them that you told your wife in front of her daughter to "take your debt and go" after promising to pay off her debts? Did you say your wife ran 2 businesses and worked a full-time job while you ran to your mommy for checks? Did you tell them the only reputation and job contract you have was the one created by your wife?

Did you say that you told your step daughter's friend that you wanted your wife gone in January only to pretend to stay committed until February? Did you say every time your wife tried to talk to you, you began yelling and pulling your hair saying it was her fault you were upset? Did you share that you told your wife to go but that her kids can stay in your house? Did you say you like black people around you so you can fulfill your white savior complex? Did you share that you are a counselor yet couldn't use your words to have a safe conversation? Did you say that you have been in the same room with your wife and completely ignore her time and time again? Did you say that you told your step daughter that her mother's sickness caused you too much stress yet you knew from day one she had an auto immune disorder? Did you say that despite all that your wife was still willing to stay and work it out with your dirty dusty spoiled incompetent narcissistic gaslighting ass? Did you tell the truth?

-curious

Dear Ex,

It hurts me every time I share a piece of our love story turned love nightmare. This is so unfair. I covered you thinking I was being a good wife, "a for better or worse wife" only to find out I was a very compliant victim. I don't even know if I was an active participant in my own abuse. Maybe your mom is right, maybe I brought this pain on myself? Maybe I deserved to be abused. Maybe I do this to all my husbands, drive them to anger and neglect? Or maybe the broken parts of me felt safe in the broken parts of you? Trauma Bonding and calling it LOVE.

Dear Ex,

Was any of it true?

Was it all lies?

I really need to know because I am going crazy trying to detangle fact from fiction.

- Investigator

Dear Ex,

Rationally, I understand how this could happen but I still don't know how this happened? I know it's not my fault but I still replay the relationship, in my mind, hoping to find the moment where you decided I was no longer your person. Or maybe I was never your person and you just pretended to be mine. How could you lie so damn good? I miss the lie sometimes. I guess it was easier for me yet harder for you. Why did you tell me it was forever if you knew I was on borrowed time? Why did you allow me to plan my life with you? Why did you work so hard to reassure me so I can release my anxiety? Why do all of that to then not love me? How could you be so cruel? I just don't understand. I wish you would tell me the truth. I don't even know if you know what truth is.

Dear Ex,

Did you know you were a narcissist before I told you? Be honest, did you?

Dear Ex

I don't know whether to regret you or not because on one hand I wish I never met you and on the other hand my life wouldn't be the same without this experience. This is not a thank you because you don't deserve it. I made you better, you've just shown me how much better I was. I upgraded you and the reward was a broken heart. You will fall fast without me and maybe you will see what everyone sees, you are a nobody with me.

Dear Ex,

What was it all for? Was this your intention? You said you never loved anyone before but was this love? I'm so confused, what do you think love is?

Dear Ex,

Why wasn't I enough for you to do better to keep me? Why wasn't I enough to fight for? You had a faithful, loyal, beautiful, sensual and sexy, educated, driven, thoughtful, committed, and freaky woman who adored you. Isn't that what men want? It doesn't make any sense. Six months into our relationship, you said, " I will fight for you". That's all I needed to hear to truly open my heart to you. You lied. Instead of fighting for me you were manipulating me until you got what you wanted. When I called you out for your unhealthy habits and unsafe behaviors, you decided it was easier to shift the blame on me and discard me. You discarded someone that enhanced your life in every way and allowed people to see you for who you wanted and pretended to be. I have no clue on who you are. I don't think you know either. You don't know what love is. You don't know what fighting for love is. For you love was a one-sided transaction where you take what you want.

How did you become this evil? Who made you this way? I pray one day I get clarity and peace in all of this. I pray one day you ask God to have mercy on your soul and you repent because God doesn't play about me and Karma is real.

Dear Ex,

Do you wake up with remorse as often as I wake up Brokenhearted? Does any part of you wish you didn't hurt me? Are you searching for understanding on how we got here? Do you feel the wrongness of your actions? Do you tell the truth when people ask you where is your wife?

Am I the only one dealing with the weight of it all?

The hardest part of this breakup is the many questions and the lack of closure. You shattered me and left me to put the pieces together. Without answers can I ever truly move on from this experience?

Dear Ex,

You really made me think you were IT. Why go to great lengths to show me you can love me correctly just to rip it all away? You tainted every innocent gesture and early courtship I may have. I won't ever feel safe enough to fall deeply in love again. I am skeptical of every compliment I receive. Why did you take that from me? Are you happy with yourself? Are you at peace with your decisions? I hope you know you broke me in a way no one has before. Was it worth all that?

-wanting answers

Dear Ex,

Was any of it true?

I really want to know.

Was it?

Dear Ex,

Last night, I dreamed of you. This is my 2nd dream of you that felt so real. The first one, you apologized to me and even though we parted you admitted it wasn't because I didn't love or care for you correctly and deeply. That dream released me from you. The dream last night though was heart wrenching. You talked to me. I was shocked because you haven't talked to me in months. We were having a casual conversation about my son and it felt so good to be connected again. At the end of the conversation, I asked if you want to hold off on the divorce so we can continue to talk. You turned towards me, with a face of disgust and said "no, I don't want to be with you". You walked away, I cried and felt so stupid. I woke up in a cold sweat.

How did this happen? How did I fall for a man like you? How in my pain, I still long for your acceptance? Did you really break my heart or did you do me a favor? Only time will tell.

I hope I will be in love again and I hope one day a man will love me and prove it with his actions consistently forever.

Lakeeya Natasha

Dear Ex,

I am not sure if this was your doing or your mother's but I am sad for you either way. I brought this concern up in premarital counseling. I cried to you, the Pastor, and the Elder sharing that I thought the success of our marriage hinged on your mother's health. At that point, I should have listened to that voice and paused the wedding until I knew if that was the truth or not. I pushed forward with encouragement from the religious leaders and your reassurance that you will fight for me always. I loved you so much and I wanted to believe you. I did not know how deep your mother wound was. I did not know how entangled your self-image was to the money she had and you did not have. At any point, did you want to really try at being independent of her?

I spoke to your first wife recently and without me sharing any part of our life, she described my experiences. She loved you too so much and the end was ugly for her as well as she could not believe what you turned in to. She also said your mother and father was the cause of your demise. She did not call it narcissism because she truly believed you had no control over your life. Do you agree? Do you have no control even now twenty years later? I do believe that narcissists aren't born, they are bred. Maybe you never had a chance because of the family you were born into? Yet, I struggle to believe that because I also wasn't born in the best of conditions. I could have succumbed to the myriad of unfortunate circumstances that life afforded me. I made a different choice. I choose to love and to dream. I choose to work hard and to help others. I choose to live in truth and follow my heart no matter how difficult. I thought that is why you loved me. I thought that was enough for me to be loveable. You made a choice not to grow up, not to fight for the people who loved you and wanted the best for you, not to work to build your own legacy, not to be self-sufficient. Your parents groomed you to always rely on them and you groomed your wives to always take care of you even when you weren't taking care of them, how is that kind, how is that loving? Your ex asked me, "Did he ever say to you that you were hostile and all you needed to be is nicer to him?" Silent tears rolled down my face. "Yes", I replied, "Oh Yes".

I knew then that I wasn't special. I was just another supply. Another victim of you. It hurt. I hurt for her as well. I hurt for all our kids that were impacted by your inability to cut your umbilical cord. Do you see it now? You were afforded another chance at a beautiful life and you forfeited it again. I don't think I will truly understand your story unless you were willing to be honest and share it with me and you chose to ghost me instead of standing in your truth. We could have worked it out if you were just honest and got help. I saw in you just what your ex-wife saw in you- a broken boy with a damaged heart and lots of potential and all we wanted to do was to love you like you deserved and be loved in turn. I will keep you in my prayers. I hate that you hurt me this way but I don't hate you.

Love,

Just another wife

Anger

Once the reality sets in, anger often follows. You might feel frustrated, angry at yourself, your ex, or the circumstances. Questions like "Why did this happen?" or "How could they leave?" may come up, and this stage is marked by intense emotions as you grapple with the situation. Rage can paralyze you as you have thoughts of doing hurtful and often illegal things make your pain known to your Ex. Jazmine Sullivan's song "Bust the Windows out your car" on repeat but you know nobody has any bail money for you so you just fantasize about going crazy just one good time.

Things I Told Myself:
"Breathe Girl, You can't go to jail"
"Fuck him and his dirty ass"
"I'm so stupid, so stupid to believe I was going to have a happy ending"
"I hope he dies so I can be a widow and not a divorcee again"
"Why would he hurt me this bad on purpose"

"It's my fault for making excuses for him for a year- this is exactly what I get"

"I don't want to date again, I hate playing these games, I should not be single right now"

Anger

Dear Ex,

Fuck You.

Sincerely,

Me

Dear Ex,

I absolutely hate you. I hate that you have me hating you. I hate that I don't want to hate everything about you. I hate everything that I loved about you. I cannot stand you literally. Every time I see you, I want to throw up. I literally would like to chop off your neck with my bear hands, I want to strangle you but do not want to go to jail. Therefore, I hate you that I can't hurt you like you hurt me. I hate the fact that I don't want to hurt you. I hate that you can hurt me and not be hurting. I hate that this is still going on. I hate that I still think about you. I hate that I still wonder what if I held on to hope so long that you will recognize what you were doing and you would change your mind and treat me better. I hate that I cry over you every single night. I hate that I can't watch a love movie. I hate that I can't read my romance books.

I hate that I become cynical. I hate that I feel like I will never find love again. I hate you for taking it from me. I truly hate you.

Always,

Your never again

Dear Ex,

I know I am better without you. I hope one day you will realize that you are worst without me. I am the best thing that could have ever happened to you. I thought you knew how blessed you were. Just like all the others, you fumbled me. You fumbled me for short term gains. Just stupid. I would have given you the world. I gave you my world. You are an asshole. If you let me go, you never deserved me in the first place. I hope you live a long time and that you choke every time my name is mentioned and it will forever be mentioned. I am about to be everything you were holding me back from being. See you were pulling me back and when you let me go you didn't recognize that I was a catapult. I am going to soar and you're going to choke. Choke on all the words you used to gaslight, manipulate, and disrespect me. Choke on all the lies you told to me and my family pretending to be a good person, pretending to be ME. I was and always will be better than you. I hope you never forget.

- your lesson

Dear Ex

Who hurt you? Someone must have hurt you that you thought it was okay to abuse me. Was it your mom? Normally it is the mom. Male Narcissists normally have an enabling mom with mental health issues. Sounds about right. Yall deserve each other! There is a place for you both.

Sincerely,

Figuring it Out

Dear Ex,

Kiss my Black Ass.

Sike, you will never do that again.

Dream about kissing my Black Ass.

Kick Rocks barefoot on chard glass.

Please and thank you,

Sincerely,

Your Never Again

Dear Ex,

You treated me like a yo-yo and I am not a game. You treated me like I was optional. You are a fucking lame!

You will see, you will regret the day you fucked up with me.

Fuck off.

From,

You know who the fuck I am

Dear Ex,

I wish I could see your Karma. I hope you experience it sooner than later. I want a front row seat with vegan butter popcorn and an organic mango smoothie.

I know I'm not supposed to but I want to watch you suffer. Yet suffering is all I want for you!

-Angry

Dear Ex,

I hope your dick cramps every time you have sex with someone else. I hope you see my face laughing at you every time you try to talk to a new woman. I hope you choke on your lies. I hope everyone sees who you really are. I hope you see it too.

I want you to regret the day you met me. I want you to wish you walked the other way.

Because I do, I wish I never met you.

- Truth Teller

Dear Ex,

You are beneath me, so fuck off. Seriously, stay away from me and mine. It's funny now I see how everyone you knew kept you at a distance or you kept them at arm's length, you didn't want them to see you. You pushed in with my friends and family masked as the knight in shining armor because we didn't know you so you could be a different person. We were your fresh supply. You are a user and that is just one way you are beneath me.

Dear Ex,

I am not a buffet. You can't pick and choose what parts of me you want. This is an all or none type of situation. All of me deserves to be loved, cared for, and protected. You tried to dismantle me and pick the parts that were easier to swallow. Silly you, the parts of me you discarded were the parts that made me the most flavorful. You can't hurt me and expect my kids to love you. You can't hurt me and expect my friends to respect you. You can't hurt me and expect by family to welcome you. They only know you because of me. You are less important than you think. You are walking around unphased because I allow you too because I could have call the

goons out for you so don't ever think you got away with it. Watch how you handle me or you will see- I will tell the world who you are and then you will have nowhere to hide.

Respectfully, stay away from me and everything attached to me because every time I see you, I want to hurt you as bad as you hurt me but I am and have always been a better person than you...count it as a blessing but I pray God gives you the lesson.

Dear Ex,

You suck!

Dear Ex,

I hope you choke every time someone says my name. Let it feel like a fish bone stuck in your throat that you can't cough enough to dislodge.

Dear Ex,

Your cock wasn't that big, I was exaggerating so you felt better about yourself. I have no desire to sleep with you again. The last few times were horrible and I realized that the sex was good because I loved you and was in love with you so if you take away my love, your dick is mediocre at best. Facts!

Dear Ex,

I can't even go to the movies; I can't even watch a sex scene without thinking of you. Don't get it twisted, I never ever want you touching me again. I don't even want another man kissing and touching me but I feel I need one to so I can delete you. I hate you for making me single again. I don't even want to be out here playing games. You abandoned me. For what!?! I didn't need another lesson of how strong I am. I am tired. I am tired of being independent. I am tired of being abused, neglected, mistreated, and overlooked. I don't want to be alone but you made it so I won't trust anything good again. Where does that leave me, with fuck boys for the rest of my life until I'm old taking care of dogs and cats? How can I truly forgive you? I pray God takes this anger from me. I pray he take this pain from me. I want to let all this go.

-Me

Lakeeya Natasha

Dear Ex,

I am glad we don't have kids together. After this divorce is final, I will never have to see you again. I am looking forward to not ever seeing your evil face again.

-ex-wife

Dear Ex,

I can't believe my life. You worked so hard to convince me that you were safe and you were forever- all to abandon me. Yes, I left you but what choices did you give me: Stay and be Abused or Leave. I mean I get it; you hedged your bets that because of my history of bad relationships and my trauma that I would be an easy pawn in your game. I know you were not expecting me to leave even though I asked you if you wanted me to leave and you said yes. It frustrates me that I didn't trust my instinct. I was blaming my anxiety when I could not relax around you and all the while it was my spirit telling me to run. You disgust me. Any person that sought out partnership with someone with the idea to manipulate and hurt is the worse type of person. The very things you said you liked about me are the very things you said annoy you at the end.

I understand now that you are envious of me and the more you were around me, the more you recognized I am a healthier person than you so you TRIED to belittle and demean me, you TRIED to break me. You are a Big Bitch! A spoiled entitled whiny ass Bitch! You thought I was a woman that came from nothing. Boy, you missed the entire memo- I am a woman that came from

EVERYTHING. My bloodline is rich. I have Shields and Merchant blood running through my veins. I have royal blood. See, when some of y'all see us, you only see the enslaved but the smart ones see the starters of all civilization. I am a Queen- it doesn't matter where a Queen is born, she is a Queen. You are a dirty ass peasant- no matter how much money you come from; you are all leeches. Your family made money from exploiting the less fortunate and you said you were not like them but YOU ARE THEM. That was my fault for believing you. If you lie with a dog, you can't get mad if you get fleas. I was trying to clean you up and you were trying to tear me down. You used me to push into uninvited spaces. I am sure I was not your first victim but I am praying that Karma makes me your last.

Dear Ex,

I hope you go on 50 first dates and they all suck. I hope you repel all the good women. I hope every time you try to spit game, they only smell shit coming out your mouth. You don't deserve another chance. You wasted your best chance. I hope your hair falls out. I hope you have erectile dysfunction and the blue pill is not covered on your insurance. I hope you chip your front tooth and the fake one doesn't quite match. I hope you choke every time you're about to tell a lie. I hope your gums turn as black as your soul. I hope you never have another happy moment until you admit what you have done to me, apologize publicly, and ask God for forgiveness. I pray the Celie curse over you- "until you do right by me, everything you think about gonna fail".

Dear Ex,

Every "hey beautiful" "good morning, Queen " "You are too good to be single" comment I receive makes me hate you. I hate dating. I hate starting over. For the first time in my life, I was completely content with spending my life with another person. I was content with you. Now I am single again. I hate you for this. I know I'm too young to write off love but you made it so easy for me to see myself as single forever. You ripped the whimsy of new love from me. You made it million times harder for those that come after you. I am trying so hard to forgive you.

Dear Ex,

Every week, I get the privilege of sitting across from hard working men. As a therapist, I hear so many things that touch my heart and as a woman, I find myself often on the verge of tears because these married men sit across from me trying to figure out ways to continue

to fight for their wives and families. These men all been married 20 plus years and have their share of troubles but all vowed to never leave their wives. These men are providers and protectors. You were a fraud. You don't hold a candle to any of them yet you swear you are better than most. You are much worse than any man I ever knew. You dropped your wife so fast, not even 2 years married and for what? You can't name one thing I have done to you. You can't say I wronged you in any way. Yet you claim, I didn't meet your needs. You are a coward. You are a boy. You are a loser. You are an abuser. How dare you counsel any man about how to interact with their family? You can't really believe your own bullshit, can you? I hope you are convicted every time you try to offer therapy to anyone because you are the most dishonest person I know and you should not be a licensed therapist, a husband, or a father!

Depression

This is often the most challenging stage. You may feel deep sadness, loneliness, and a sense of loss for the future you had imagined. It's common to withdraw, feel exhausted, or struggle with feelings of hopelessness during this period. Now, this stage can be tricky and dangerous if you have an history of depression or currently managing depressive symptoms. A painful breakup can resurface feelings of inadequacy and unworthiness really quick. You find yourself isolating from people trying to support you. The sadness becomes a weighted blanket and it becomes a struggle to do simple tasks like getting out of bed, taking a shower, or eating. You will be going to work as a shell of yourself, just going through the motions, or you are calling off more than usual. When self-injurious thoughts or fantasies about your death seems like a good way to escape, this depression can get scary. If you have thoughts of ending your life, please know your life is more than this moment and your pain will not end with your passing but it will be transferred to all you leave behind. **Please get help by going to your nearest hospital/ crisis** center & call or text 988 the National Suicide and Crisis Lifeline.

Things I told myself:
"I can't do this anymore"
"Just stop taking your meds- it will look natural"
"This pain hurts too much, I can't breathe"
"What if I just got in a car accident- nah, that would hurt and I might not die"
"No one will ever love me"
"This was your last chance Keeya, it's over, you can't get married again"
"Three strikes you out"
"Why won't he talk to me, why he don't want me"

Depression

Dear Ex,

How do you sleep at night? I'm truly asking. How do you sleep at night? Sound asleep snoring while I toss and turn in pain. How do you sleep at night? What kind of monster? Can people sleep well after they torment someone? How can you sleep well? You used to love me.

How do you sleep well? You are losing me. It doesn't bother you at all? Was any part real for you? Because I couldn't get up until noon today, I didn't have strength to take a shower so I just washed my face from the tears from the night before. My body aches, my head hurts and I am exhausted. Yes, I have to get up. I have children counting on me. I have people counting on me. I am living one day at a time.

How do you sleep? Can you give me that parting advice?

- Exhausted

Dear Ex,

I can't sleep.

I stay up as long as I can. This is so hard. I loved you so much. I just don't understand.

How did you to hurt me so well? I loved you so much.

I feel like I'm going crazy. Why would you do this to me?

What did I do to deserve to this? I am struggling to get through my day. All because I loved it when I thought you loved me. Someone who promised to take care of me, to protect me, someone that assured me only a few months ago that he wasn't leaving me. Now I can't sleep because you became a nightmare when you once was the dream. I am struggling to breathe. I am full of pain. My body aches, my head hurts. I am so tired. I can't keep the tears out my eyes.

I really don't understand. I really did love you. I really, really did love you. I wanted to be loved. I wanted to love you. And you broke me.

You broke me in a way that I don't know, if I'll I ever get fixed? I do not even want to live. I survived so much and now I have to survive this. I slept next to a man who woke up every day and made me breakfast for two years, only to discard me like a piece of trash.

You helped me love you. You helped me make others believe in true love. You made me believe, only to cut me so deep.

I'm trying to do all the things I know to do yet at the end of the night, when everything is Quiet, the silence is echoing the emptiness of my bed and in my heart. It's too much. I'm glad I don't drink because if I did, I'd be drowning. The painkillers kill no pain. There's no high high enough to float me above the sorrow, I feel every day. You took love from me. You took trust from me. I don't know how I will ever forgive you and I know I have to because I'm a good person. I still have to be a good person so I'll pray for you.

I prayed that you ask God for forgiveness because only God can help you.

Dear Ex,

God gave you something really special.

It was not enough for you. You were given a prize and you played me like a toy. I am so hurt. You are not deserving of my tears. You can pretend with whoever you like.

Your heart is cold and black.

You're not fooling anyone.

People will see who you are. I hope one day you see who you are. I'm sad because I know I even if you change, I will never be with you again. You forfeit your chance because I will never trust you again. That's what makes me so sad.

I wanted so hard to be your wife. I did what you wanted, what you desired and for what?

I can't breathe.

How did I not see that coming?

You hurt my feelings. You hurt my kids. You made them cry.

You loved me in front of them and hated me in front of them. I hate that you even got to know them. I wish I'd never met you. You took more from me than I ever taken from you.

What is in my future? Since you know so much. What is the end game? What was your plan? Did you succeed? Who's next on your list? I'm horrified, I'm terrified to know that. Snot running down my face. Nose stopped up. Glasses speckled with salty tears. You're not a good person. You are a liar. You are such a good liar.

Sincerely,

Broken

Dear Ex,

How are you? I truly wish I knew. I fantasize that you are as sad as me but logic tells me you have moved on just fine. If you were as distraught as me you would have reached out by now. You were the one to dismantle our relationship so you would need to be the one to reach out at this point. While together, I cried and begged for you to communicate with me, to fight for us with me but instead you fought me. I have a moment of sadness every day. I can't watch a rom com without crying and they used to be my favorite type of movies and yes, I know, you know that about me. I remember begging you to watch movies I liked yet the compromise was always watch what you wanted- action or drama. I just liked sitting next to you. Didn't you notice that? You took me for granted, didn't you? Do you know that? Probably not. I can't look at a couple without a puddle of tears welling up in my eyes. I used to love LOVE. I used to be excited at the thought that my person would come one day. I thought it was you. You stole that from me. I can't even cry right now because I have things to do. I hope you are as miserable as I am and if you are not miserable than I guess this was all for the best because anyone who lost me should be devastated.

Sincerely,

Broken-hearted

Dear Ex,

My heart hurts, I hope yours do too.

- Sad

Dear Ex,

Why did you fumble me? I am a catch. I am a great catch and I let you catch me. I ran from love for so long and I slowed down for you. I compromised for you. I learned new things for you. I healed so I could feel worthy of the love I thought you were giving me. It was all a lie. I was so happy. What a mess you've made. You forfeited the greatest love story you could ever have. I loved you so much. I gave you so much. Why wasn't that enough? I was and am more than enough and because of you, I will question every good intentioned man that comes next. I am so mad at you for that. No closure. No truth. Just lies and heartache. Confusion and sleepless nights. I was a good girl. I am a great woman. I was great to you. We would have been great together. We could have had a happily ever after. You messed up. I was your ONE.

Dear Ex,

I am tired of crying. I am tired.

I didn't deserve this.

I'm miserable and you moved on.

I cannot wait until I move on too.

- Sadly Yours

Dear Ex,

You destroyed our family. Did you even think about the kids? Did you think that

hurting their mom and stepmom would hurt them? Did you think that hurting me would change their lives? Did you think your behaviors will shape their view of love and marriage? Either you did and didn't care about blowing up their lives or you didn't think about them at all. Either way, you were selfish and unkind to us all.

Lakeeya Natasha

Dear Ex,

I hate that I have to pretend to be okay when people call to check on me. I am tired of complaining, crying, and venting about you. It's been months and I am tired of hearing myself so I stopped the self-loathing responses. I now say, "I'm okay, I'm fine, I'm good" because if I am not in that moment I will be soon. I am tired of people feeling sorry for me. They should feel sorry for you for losing me.

Dear Ex,

I hate that I am still crying over you.

I am done talking about you. I hate that we still have people and bills that connect us. I can't wait to the day when you disappear from my mind and my heart.

Dear Ex,

I feel the pain every day. It feels like yesterday when you just stopped loving me. You literally stopped talking to me. Ghosted me in my own home. The silence became so deafening I had to leave to regain my sanity. It's been a week since I moved out. I guess it was never my home. Now, I am doing all the things I would tell my clients to do. I am getting up. Eating clean. Exercising. Praying. Going to church. Resting. Hanging out with positive people. Journaling. Meditating. Yet as soon as I stop moving, here comes grief to put me in a choke hold again. I can't breathe. I thought my last ex was my last ex. I am so mad at you. What have you done to me...

Dear Ex,

I remember as a teenager sending little boyfriends letters with song lyrics to share my feelings. I smile thinking how in my feelings I thought I was not knowing how deep love really was and what true heartbreak felt like. You are the one who showed me both. I wanted to share this Adele song with you because I have been listening on repeat. She captured exactly how I feel:

Woman Like Me-

You're driving me away, give me a reason to stay

I want to be lost in you, but not in this way

Don't think you quite understand who you have on your hands

How can you not see just how good for you I am?

I know that you've been hurt before, that's why you feel so insecure

I begged you to let me in, 'cause I only want to be the cure

If you don't choose to grow, we ain't ever gonna know

Just how good this could be

I really hoped that this would go somewhere

Complacency is the worst trait to have, are you crazy?

You ain't never had, ain't never had a woman like me

It is so sad, a man like you could be so lazy

Consistency is the gift to give for free, and it is key

To ever keep, to ever keep a woman like me

All you do is complain about decisions you make

How can I help lift you if you refuse to activate the life that you truly want?

I know it's hard, but it's not

We come from the same place, but you will never give it up

It's where they make you feel powerful

That's why you think I make you feel small

But that's your projection, it's not my rejection

I put my heart on the line for the very first time

Because you asked me to, and now you've gone and changed your mind

But loving you was a breakthrough

I saw what my heart can really do

Now some other man will get the love I have for you

'Cause you don't care, oh-oh-oh

Complacency is the worst trait to have, are you crazy?

You ain't never had, ain't never had a woman like me

It is so sad, a man like you could be so lazy

Consistency is the gift to give for free, and it is key

To ever keep, to ever keep a woman like me

A woman like me (one more time)

Complacency (woman like me) is the

worst trait to have (woman like me)

Are you crazy? (Woman like me)

You ain't never had, ain't never had a woman like me (woman like me)

It is so sad, a man like you could be so lazy (woman like me)

Consistency is the gift to give for free...

Source: Musixmatch

Songwriters: Adele Laurie Blue Adkins / Dean Wynton Josiah Cover

Woman Like Me lyrics © Melted Stone Publishing Ltd.

- a real Woman with real feelings

Lakeeya Natasha

Dear Ex,

It is hard to look at you now. I get really anxious when I think I will see you. My stomach be in knots. I hate that we work together. I missed so many days over you. You took something I loved and corrupted it. I pray God will replace this income sooner than later so I will never have to see you again once the divorce is final. I hope the judge awards me pain and suffering so I can sever business ties from you once in for all. You jeopardized my businesses and reputation with your foolishness. I hope everyone sees the fraud you are and you can't get work until you do the work on yourself. By the way, I won't be in today.

Peace.

- your ex-business partner

Dear Ex,

Last night, I had a dream that in a court room filled with my friends and family, you admitted it all. You told the truth. You told them that you deceived me from the beginning. You told them that you saw me as an easy prey. You told them how you groomed me. You didn't expect me to be so genuine and that agitated you. You said you tried everything to break my spirit but it couldn't be broken so you decided to let me go. I forgave you and prayed for you and told you that I wished you Healing and a closeness with God. I released you and you released me in peace. I felt vindicated. I woke up with such a heaviness because I doubt that would ever happen. I frustrate myself wanting accountability from you. I pray, one day, I won't need closure yet until that day comes, I will offer myself grace and search for a path for me to offer you forgiveness without apology.

-Dreamer

Lakeeya Natasha

Dear Ex,

I know that the wound you caused will take time to heal. It hurts so much. I'm not sad because we broke up because I experienced breakups before. Each breakup stung but it was necessary because I wasn't who I needed to be. I wanted something from someone else that I was not willing to give myself. This hurts because I was who I needed to be. I gave you a balanced love. I did not require you to do anything I wasn't willing to do yet you demanded so much from me while withholding the things you knew I needed, things you gave me in the beginning- love, acceptance, security, reassurance, care. This hurts so much because you knew exactly how to love me, showed me that love, them dangled that love as a prize I can earn back with good behavior. How cruel.

I loved you so much. You literally had it all. You had a faithful, healed, whole, secure, beautiful, sexy, sensual, smart, driven, caring, and super affectionate loving woman that was ready and eager to create an empire with you. You had a Queen and literally treated her like a dog. Once I realized you wanted me to earn your scraps, I realized you were no longer my person. You were the dog. You were the con artist. I never deserved this. I did nothing to you to deserve this. The fact that you cannot take accountability is so fucked up and that is what makes this so difficult. You are a narcissist, of course it can't be your fault. I made you do it.

My heart yearns for your honesty. My mind craves proper closure that I will never get from you. Yet my spirit guides me in truth. Your actions and inaction are my closure. I am truly devastated yet God is sustaining me with my daily bread. You will soon see how I will rise from the ashes once again. You will never doubt me or my God again.

Dear Ex,

Shattered Mirrors, that is all we are.
You broke us.

-Devastated

Dear Ex,

Why do I have to tell people we broke up?

Why can't you say how you dismantled us?

Why do you have to be a coward even in the end? If you didn't want to be with me, why didn't you stand on that instead of driving me crazy until I had no choice but to leave? Now, I am the one that had to leave and also have to explain what you have done. How is that fair?

-Tired

Dear Ex,

I don't understand why I am still crying over you. This grief is so real, it is unbearable. Some moments I just want to fast forward my life and some moments I feel I am better off gone. How could you have done this to me? What did I do to deserve this? I am doing all the things I know to do but I don't want to do any of it. I just want to disappear. I wish I could erase you from my memory. Erase the last 4 years.

Dear Ex,

I would have died for you and all I asked for you is to live for me. I didn't think I was asking for too much.

Dear Ex,

I don't want you back but I didn't sign up to be single. This is so unfair. You just

glide on to the next one and I am still trying to get my footing in this new life. How can you just erase all the love we had and the memories we made? It is no way this was all make believe. The idea of dating again makes me nauseous. Why did you hurt me like this? Why didn't you just leave me alone? You are gone and I am trying to pick up the pieces of my shattered heart.

Dear Ex,

Painful is not the word. Grief is the gift we get for loving someone but I was hoping we had at least 40 years before we had to say goodbye to each other. We didn't even get a formal goodbye. I feel I deserved at least the truth and a thoughtful goodbye. I never desired closure so much in my life. I really loved you. You hurt me so bad. This hurts so bad.

Dear Ex,

I spoke to a guy today who said whoever lost me should be upset. I smiled and immediately cried. Everyone sees my value but who I decide to partner with. All I wanted is someone who prioritizes me as much as I prioritize them. All I wanted was a safe place to be myself. All I wanted was fertile grounds to grow my vision and multiple our dreams together. I gave you so much. I gave you the best parts of me and that wasn't enough for you to treat me better. It wasn't enough to get you to honor your vows and love me unconditionally. What is the point of being a good girl and a great wife when men don't want to be husbands? I am devastated and tired of trying to make people love me. I am deserving of someone like me. Clearly, that is not you. You were such a good pretender. You are just another man who didn't know what he had. I am sad for all of you. You fumbled a gift from above when you dropped me. You may find another supply but you will never find another me.

Dear Ex,

I wanted to be your person because you were my person. Now, I wake up each day wondering if my person was even real. Was my selection of you based on what I wanted to see versus what you were showing me or telling me? If I loved you in truth, how could my love be a lie? If I thought you were my person and you weren't, did I miss my person by being with you? Will I recognize him when he comes for me? Will I accept my person's love and commitment or will the brokenness and doubt you created cause me to panic and attack. I thought I was done the search. I thought I was done with the chase. I thought me choosing you made me enough to be chosen by you. I am having such a hard time accepting that the person I thought I would grow and heal with caused the deepest scars then discarded me so nonchalantly. This just can't be my life. What did I do to deserve this?

Dear Ex,

After every nice chat with a new man, I get so sad. Why am I here? Why am I such a great catch and no one wants to keep me? What is the point? What was the point? To prove you can uproot someone's life and cause pain...

I am praying that the pain you caused me won't impact me finding my forever love. I am deserving of love yet your actions created so much doubt in my heart. I am tired of crying over this. I am not crying for you. I am crying over your patterns of behavior and ultimately your discard that led me to feel lost, confused, and unsure of my future I was just so certain of.

Dear Ex,

I know that no closure is the closure but it hurts so bad. I can't tell you how bad I'm hurting because I know you will dismiss my feelings and it will only hurt more. So, I struggle every day not calling you, texting you, emailing you. So, I struggle not riding passed what once was our home and busting all your windows out. So, I struggle not telling everyone I know and meet how degrading you were. So, I struggle with the truth while you get to continue living your lie. I am a good person who loved you. So, I struggle trying not to drown in my tears, trying not to be crushed by my pain. I struggle to do simple tasks. I struggle to eat. I struggle to sleep. I struggle to wake. I struggle and you just move on. My punishment for finally letting down my guard and giving love a chance. I guess my struggle will have to be my closure because if I'm struggling it means what you did to me was real. Real love doesn't do what you have done to me so I know it wasn't true love, you weren't my soul mate, you are not the Yang to my Yin...you are just a loser, a fraud, an abuser, a narcissist.

Dear Ex,

I've been hurt before but never heartbroken. You broke my heart then wrote on the divorce papers that you did nothing wrong. How is it possible that you feel no wrong when all I feel is pain. If I could have bet my life that we would grow old together, I would have. Now I live in uncertainty. Now every interaction with a man feels like a red flag. Every compliment or gesture feels like love bombing. Every kiss feels like a kiss goodbye. Every time someone says "Keeya, I like you", I think my ex used to like me too. I know I have to move on. You moved on while we were married and I am still struggling to move on as a divorced woman. What is the point? All I am is a girl wanting to be loved, cared for by a man willing to give the love I desire. Everyone wants my love, my care, my concern, my body yet no one wants ME. I wish just one of my exes could admit this truth and put me out my misery. I wish you could have told me the truth and tell the same world I put you on a pedestal in front of, that you were wrong. Tell them that I'm am loveable and you were wrong.

- Broken-hearted

Dear Ex

I wish God gave me a good husband. All I wanted is to feel loved and protected. You took advantage of my need to be cared for. You took advantage of my trauma wounds. All I needed was a good husband. All you gave me is another heartache. Pain so unbearable, I have to remind myself to breathe. An ache so deep, I have to force myself to live each day. I deserved true love. I gave you all of me and you lied to my face, in front of our children, our family, and our friends

when you said you would be my husband for the rest of our lives. Instead, you killed me. You murdered my belief in love. You crushed my soul. You filed for divorce and denied any wrong doing. I didn't even get your accountability at the end. The statement that you did nothing wrong was a dagger to my heart. How could you do this to me and walk away like you've done nothing? I am trying to rebuild with the shattered pieces of me. I truly wish I never met you. I wish God gave me a good husband.

-a good wife

Acceptance

Eventually, there's an understanding and acceptance that the relationship is over. This doesn't mean you're happy about it, but you come to terms with the breakup and begin to move forward. It's the beginning of emotional healing and the ability to envision life beyond the relationship. The stages aren't always linear, and you might experience them in different orders or revisit certain stages. Grieving a breakup takes time and self-compassion, but eventually, acceptance opens the door to new growth, healing, and the possibility of future relationships. There is peace in acceptance yet this stage is deceptive. One wrong turn (a memory on your timeline, a new person you have to share the news to, a milestone day approaches, navigating online dating, a flashback of a good or bad time) and you are right back in the throes of one of the other stages. Acceptance is like your favorite auntie that you don't see that often but when you see her, you embrace her and tell her about your plans and she is so happy for you then when it is time for her to leave you wonder if you will see her again...you will. Just as grief visits you, joy and peace will visit you too. Honor the entire process. Honor all your feelings. You may always grieve some aspect of the old relationship but you won't always be swallowed up by grief. You will live again.

Things I told myself:
"You will be okay"
"You gained so much from that partnership and it wasn't ever supposed to be forever"
"He was your test and you passed"
"You were vulnerable and he knew that, it is not your fault"
"God has forgiven you and is with you"
"Keep praying for him"
"Your future will include love, real love, just watch"

Acceptance

Dear Ex,

I don't regret the love I gave you because clearly you needed it. I don't regret our time together because I learned so much about myself. I am so very proud of me. If you were a test to see if I healed, I got an A+. I never questioned my worth in all of this. I knew what I deserved from day one and when you'd shown me that you are less than that, I exited despite all the love and desire I had for you because I finally realized how much I loved myself. I am so in love with myself that I will never ever settle again. For that I want to thank you. I will sleep soundly again. I will laugh and love again just not with you. I leave today. I am leaving agape love with you yet your access is forever denied. You will never enjoy me again. I wish you Wellness. I wish you Healing. I wish you Truth. I wish you find God in all of this and repent. I wish that we part ways in peace and that you let me go in kindness.

Love

Dear Ex,

I slept good without you. Real good. Yesterday, it finally clicked. You were not the one. You were the preparer. You prepared my heart, mind, and soul for the next season of my life. Your love prepared me for a soft life. You've shown me that the love I always wanted was available for me and I learned how to lean into that. I learned to trust. I learned to submit. I learned to embrace joy and romantic love. I learned that I am a force to be reckoned with. A force of beauty and light. I attract beautiful things, I attract beautiful people, I attract beautiful experiences.

You prepared my mind by showing me that detachment is a part of the process. If I attract what is beautiful that means I repel what is ugly. I used to believe that people rejecting me was a sign that I am not enough and your rejection allowed me to shift my mind into understanding that I have to experience rejection to experience the pure. Everyone that rejected me including you served a purpose while they were in my life. I thank God for all of you. I learned that who I am is not a reflection of who is attached to me but who is attached to me is a reflection of who I am. My relationship with you allowed me to be curious about me. I explored what made me so loveable and I fell in love with her. I needed you for that and you'd done that for me so I don't regret our relationship at all.

Even as things fell apart, my instinct was to chase the old

feelings and hurt myself to keep you, I knew that was not my destiny. I had to stand in truth and let the lies flee. You fled from me so fast I suffered whiplash. I didn't understand your motives or your moves but I understood the only move I had to make was to move on and let go. See, before you courted me I already surrendered my life to God. I told God if He allowed me to leave that last season, I would surrender my will for His. In that moment, I transformed but I couldn't quite see it yet. I only seen the thorn in my side. I walked into our relationship wounded and thirsty. You quenched that thirst. You quenched my thirst because you saw my thorn as a weakness. You saw that thorn as an opportunity to manipulate me.

You were plotting on me. All the while, I was growing stronger in my weakness by being vulnerable, transparent, and inspiring to others. While you were so focused on my thorn, you could not see who I have become. God knew. I saw and when you finally saw me, you were intimidated. Your interactions shown your cowardice. It's funny because you tried to break me but I was already broken and built back together, in such a way, that I am unbreakable. I am able to adjust my expectations and my responses based on who is in front of me not who I

want you to be.

I now see you as my test. I got to ask myself how healed are you? are you going to walk by faith or fear? are you going to chase or attract? are you enough to be happy? Clearly, since I was able to walk away from you; you, me, and everyone else knows my answers and God is pleased with me. I forgive you for all the pain you caused me in this past year. I release you in the spirit of love. I will be forever grateful for you because loving you allowed me to unapologetically love myself. In this season, I was redeemed from all my feelings of unworthiness and inadequacy. I leave you in peace and I pray you find peace. I will be more than fine. My mind is renewed, heart is restored, and soul is refreshed. I lost nothing.

So grateful,

Queen

Dear Ex,

You had me fooled. You are a narcissist. If your plan all along was to break me, you almost won. You had me questioning my worth and my sanity. Yet, you underestimated me. I wasn't as broken as you thought. God kept me. My not-so-secret weapon. You used to say how much

you admired my faith now I'm sure it irritates your demons. I will always be light. I will always live in the light. I could have been your light but you chose darkness. Your loss, not mine.

Peace & Blessings,

Queen

Dear Ex,

I watched my first romcom since our breakup and I felt hope. I carried heavy items up 3 flights of steps. I hung up my own curtains, the drill was tricky but I got it done. I made a meal for one. I danced around my new place listening to my friends "Getting over Fuck Boys 101" Playlist on Spotify. I slept in my Queen bed stretched out and I did not need your body for comfort. I slept soundly. I woke up took my dog for a walk and joined a yoga class. I am many steps closer to being over you. I am grateful for these moments. I will be okay. I am finding my happy again.

Sincerely,

Once yours

Dear Ex,

Of course I blocked you. It's over.

Bye!

Dear Ex,

I still pray for you. I still wish you well. Even if you are not mine, I want you to be okay. I want you to find Mental, Physical, and Spiritual Wellness. I want you to find peace. You taught me that I can't be someone's peace that didn't have peace to begin with. I hope you heal. As I am healing, the less I think of you in a romantic sense. I don't long for you in my bed. I sleep soundly. I can no longer romanticize our relationship because you caused me so much pain in the end. I pray you don't hurt any other person. I pray you no longer hurt yourself because losing me was you hurting yourself. You had a faithful and devoted partner who would have loved you forever. I don't miss you but I do miss her. I miss her big smiles and overjoyed heart. I will smile again. I will love again. I will experience bliss and good sex again. I am in pursuit of my happy place again and I pray you will find your happy place too.

Sincerely,

Love

Dear Ex,

You taught me so many things but none more valuable than to trust my instinct. You strengthen my awareness of myself and others as I had to become hyper aware of your moods. You strengthen my love for myself every time you isolated me. You strengthen my determination every time you told me I could not do something. You strengthen my inner peace and ability to maintain joy every time you made my life a living hell. Despite the pain you caused and you are causing me, I am grateful for our time together because I would not be this version of myself with you.

Thankfully,

Better without you

Dear Ex,

You got me back in these streets. It's going to be a fun summer, thanks!

-Hot girl summer loading

Dear Ex,

You missed your opportunity to get me back. I began dreaming and planning about my post-YOU life and it looks and feels amazing! I've been practicing my answers for the Kendra G show so by this time next year, I'll be entertaining new suitors- having fun, exploring new things, traveling, and having great sex! Your window of opportunity closed because I'm now excited to see what is next and I'm hopeful that it will be everything I need it to be.

Love,

Hopeful Romantic

Dear Ex,

I prayed for you. I didn't want to but I know that I must pray for your soul and for what you have done to me. May you find God, repent, and find peace before your ending.

Love,

Mrs. Peace

Lakeeya Natasha

Dear Ex,

I'm a therapist. How the hell did I marry a therapist and had no idea he was a narcissist? I am a therapist and another therapist had me contemplating suicide. You almost won. I wonder if you know how demented you are? You had me fooled and I helped you fool others because I praised you and put you on this pedestal. You lied to all of us. Our whole relationship, wedding, and marriage was a sham. You are a damn good liar. Your love bombing was top tier. You waited until after the wedding, right before the first anniversary before you shown any signs. But like I said, you almost won. You tried the wrong woman. I called you out every time. I said right to your face stop trying to gaslight me. I told you that you have to treat me better and pursue me like you'd done in the beginning. The crazy thing is while I was saying these things I didn't know all of that was a lie. I didn't know you were a narcissist then. I thought you were just going through something and needed a reminder. I thought my love and commitment would be enough to bring you back to yourself. Little did I know that all the love stuff was the phase, this was who you are.

I saw you completely, without your mask on, for the first time February 10, 2024 and I could never unsee what I saw that night. I think we both knew then it was over over. You knew you couldn't manipulate me anymore and I knew I would never see you the same. From that day, you made my life a living hell. I couldn't believe you were still counseling others like nothing was happening while I had to cancel clients and take time off work. You are a truly evil person. Worse than the devil because the devil doesn't pretend to be good. I told my therapist that you use people to make you feel better about yourself because you are hallowed, truly empty inside. You were wearing me like a coat so when people seen you, they saw me however my skin doesn't fit you, you grew uncomfortable because I am what you were pretending to be all these years. I am a good person and good soul and it agitated the hell out your demons. You could not keep up the act because who I am was never an act. This is me. SO, YOU LOSE MR. NARCISSIST! YOU LOSE! I WILL LIVE AGAIN. I WILL LOVE AGAIN. I WILL THRIVE AGAIN. YOU ALMOST WON BUT BRANDY SAID "ALMOST DOESNT COUNT"

Love,

The Winner

Dear Ex,

I made my own oatmeal and it tasted better than yours.

I realized in that moment; I would be just fine.

All smiles,

Keeya

Dear Ex,

Each day I am away from you is a day I feel more restored, more peaceful, and safer. You pretended to be a safe place for me but you were really a bear trap covered in honey. You made me feel like you were my happy place. Being without you, made me realize that I carry my happy place within me. It is wherever I am. Whatever space I feel safe enough to be my authentic self. I know you are shocked how fast I left you when I saw the writing on the wall. I know you thought my love for you and my history of trauma was going to keep me in bondage and as your play thing for a little while longer. Nope, while you were busy manipulating and plotting, I was over there healing.

I thought I was healing to be able to adequately receive your love that I felt I deserved only to find out that I was healing so when I needed to, I could choose me and my love over a facade. There was a moment, maybe even moments that I felt there could be a way back to you- if you got help, if you were honest, if you took accountability. As each day goes by, I recognized that will never happen because it would take me years maybe decades before I felt safe with you again and I don't have that type time. I rather be peaceful alone than to be dancing and prancing around someone I have to prove to daily that I am worthy of your loving. I want you to heal yet not for me. I want you to heal for you, your kids, and your future victims, I mean partners.

To be honest, the hardest part of me leaving you is having to tell everyone you are a fraud. I felt so embarrassed because I truly displayed you as the lover of my soul. That hurt because you know I hate liars and I hate lying more than anything and you made me a liar or so I thought.

Now, I acknowledge that you were the only liar in this relationship. My love and commitment had only one stipulation- don't abuse it. Once the love bombing turned to devaluation, I gave you a chance to autocorrect. You didn't and I moved on in truth and with truth and love and with love. What I was not expecting is how fast you discarded me. You began to ice me out and treat me like a stranger. Now you are the stranger to me. I am so much better without you yet thanking you for giving me this experience that will help me, help others, in a new and deeper way. I will not be silenced. You did not win. I sleep in peace every night now and I wake up with new purpose every day. In case you were wondering, I am safe, I am secure, I am free, I am happy, I am looking forward to finalizing the divorce, I am hopeful for fun, love, and good sex in my near future. I guess you didn't groom me that well.

Peace & Blessings,

Keeya

Dear Ex,

You were good at pretending. You should go to acting school. You would be the top of your class. I know you hate me because I see you. You tried to be me but couldn't keep up the act. Laughable to think I ever thought you could be on my level.

Jokes on you!

Dear Ex,

I told you on February 10, 2024, that your vibrations were so low that I was growing tired of fluttering down there with you. You looked at me with a ghost face and wide eyes as if I said something you already knew. You told me shrooms were healing but you didn't expect them to transform my sight. That night I saw you, your spirit was dark as night, you were a pig wallowing in your own shit with hoofs for feet, you were big as a hog yet your energy screamed abandoned piglet. I stood above you looking down at you and I heard so clearly "this is not who you are Keeya, he is not like you, look at him". I didn't tell you then the images I saw but I did share with you the message thinking you would change your posture with me. I thought that night of revelation and great sex would have saved our relationship but it actually ended it.

Dear Ex,

"My Vibrations are too high for you. I get that now." Said the butterfly to the worm

Dear Ex

I thought I found the real thing, real love but you ain't shit. The love I found was from me. My love for myself commanded me to walk away from your trifling ass.

-self-love Queen

Dear Ex,

You are not even original. You tried to weaponize your mental health, my trauma, my physical health, and my Christianity. My other husbands did the same thing. Yet I was prepared this time around, I guess with all the practice I was ready for this test. I called it out immediately every

single time you tried it. I smile every time I remember the night I said, "you are not gonna gaslight me". Do you remember your face? If it could your head would have spun because your eyes were bugged out and you started growling like the demon you are. I wasn't scared of you though; it was like God was right behind me and a multitude of angels were next to me because you looked truly terrified of me.

I don't know how many times you used your depression as an excuse for ignoring me, neglecting me, and even being mean towards me. Your mom and daughter also did the same by saying, "Well, it's just his depression he will come back around, just give him space", "Well, his depression used to be much worse, he treats you so much better than the others", "He never loved anyone before so be patient with him". I know your mom was a willing and aware participant but I truly believe your daughter was recruited without even knowing because she was also manipulated to idolize you and make excuses for your poor parenting and lack of love.

You picked me because I am an empath, a therapist, and a Christian. You knew my capacity to create a safe space for you by offering understanding, compassion, and forgiveness. You hit the jackpot. I was the perfect supply. Or so you thought, lol. I was an easy prey in the love bombing phase because my last relationship left me so desperate for love and attention. I was so thirsty so I lapped it all up. However; you failed to see that I was not broken, I was recovering and there is a huge difference. The love you pretended to give was what I always knew I deserved so as I soaked it up, I got stronger. I got so strong that when you started moving differently, I noticed it and adjusted. First by giving you space to go through what you were going through and used that time to nourish me. Second, I tried to address it with you and every time you found a way to make your behaviors my fault. Lastly, you were making me feel unsafe and made it impossible for me to live with you so I separated myself. You never got a chance to truly devalue me because I was fully aware of my value.

By the end, you were grasping for straws, using the very things you said you admire about me against me. You threw my trauma in my face. You threw my grief in my face. I was in so much pain and you emotionally kicked me when I was already down. You told me that I was "full of trauma", another moment I will never forget. You kept telling me and our kids that I was constantly in fight or flight mode over the past year yet never acknowledged what triggered such a trauma response in me- You!

I couldn't believe a therapist could be so emotionally abusive to his wife because I guess narcissists go where the supply.

DearEx,

What better job to have but a counselor to feel superior to others. I had to educate you so much on trauma triggers and responses because what you said made no sense. I wasn't fighting you and I was not fleeing you- I stood in confidence that you were wrong and I did it assertively and you labeled me hostile. You tried to recruit "my friends" to view me as hostile and passive aggressive. You were trying to silence me and I'm sorry, not sorry- your plan failed. I was no longer ashamed of my trauma or imprisoned by it. Self-Love freed me...you were too late for that tactic. You had to catch me 5 years before.

You tried to weaponize my auto immune disorder. You started as a supportive lover and caregiver almost overly concerned with my health and getting me better. Then after marriage, the disparaging remarks began. "You sick again." "You're in a flare up right." "It's always something with you." I began hiding when I didn't feel well and when I finally was in so much pain, I couldn't hide it, you began to say you were sick too and couldn't help me. You went from intentionally loving me back to good health and giving me a safe place to recover to attacking me for needing the same things. Yet, in the past year, you got a thrill from seeing me down. I would hear you say to others, " yeah she sick again". You put a commode next to our bed so I didn't have to walk far during a flare up yet I had to empty it. When I felt better and wanted to remove the commode from our bedroom you got upset. You used me having a commode to get you a pee container and you stopped getting up to go to the bathroom. The day I moved out I took a picture of your "pee container " by the side of your bed still while I was able to put the commode back in the garage months before. I realized your lack of cleanliness and your emotional abuse was making me sick. I took a picture of your spaces before I left so if you ever deny it, I have proof. I left our marital bed in February and the room was never cleaned since. My new space now is what I wanted, a sacred place where I can rest, create, recover, and inspire so thank you for pushing me out.

And finally, you tried like many people before you to use my faith against me. You used to say I was the only real Christian you knew. You used to say my faith inspires you. That quickly turned into my faith was an annoyance and inconvenience. You dismissed my beliefs and began mocking God and I told you several times to stop, for your sake not mine because I have a healthy fear of the Lord so I was worried for you.

A Christian wife suffers so much. The standards and expectation to never leave a man that hurts you yet I never hear stories of men challenged to stay with women who cheated, disrespected, or neglected them countless times. We as women are made to feel like a failure if you walk away from a relationship after the first sign of mistreatment. For many, I will be labeled as a quitter because I divorced 3 husbands but I am not a quitter, I will persevere until healthy love shows up for me. This time Love did show up- self-love showed up. My God doesn't want me to have a struggle love. If I am to suffer it is for righteousness sake. I was led, by fear, to stay in my other marriages well pass the expiration date but this time there was no fear in sight, just faith. God guided me effortlessly away from you. I am so grateful.

Your weaponization tactics were a bust. I truly pray you stop preying on innocent women. There are many women out there that would love to be your "sex maid" or shared your same kinks if you are honest, it could be beneficial for you both- it's called a sex worker. Never trapped someone with the facade of love when you know all you really wanted was a maid you could have sex with. Like I said, not original. Loser. You mess with the wrong one but I'm sure you know this by now.

Dear Ex,

Why aren't you telling people we are over? Don't think you have a chance to double back because I never go back- you know this right!?!

- the Cut Off Queen

Dear Ex,

Please stop playing the victim. If hurting me doesn't hurt you, you didn't love me. If not speaking to me doesn't hurt you, you don't love me. If you don't care about my physical, emotional, or financial safety, you never loved me. If you don't love me, what did you expect me to do? I need to be loved and I deserve to be loved completely and consistently. It was a hard pill to swallow but I had to leave when you proved to me that you did not love me.

Dear Ex,

I know now that I am absolutely better off without you and your inconsistent love. When people say the word unfaithful, they normally mean cheating on someone yet faithful means to remain loyal and steadfast. You were not faithful to me. My vows were to someone that didn't exist. I married your persona and you divorced me. When I got the papers and it was dated only a few days after I moved out shown me you never had any intention to try to work it out with me. I am loyal and I am steadfast and if I cannot find that in another person, I will marry myself. Thank you for showing me, that everything I wanted in a partner, I already had inside of me. I love myself so much more now so the expectations of anyone saying they love me should feel similar to how I love myself- honest, true, kind, loving, compassionate, understanding, and someone that adores and accepts me for me.

- A grateful Ex-wife

Dear Ex,

You underestimated me. Laughable. If you underestimated me, you never knew me because this is who I am. I don't stay down for long. God takes all my mess and makes a blessing out of it EVERY SINGLE TIME. I was always destined to be great and to help great numbers of people. This is why I had to walk through so many fires but never smelled like smoke. The Way Maker made me a path setter, which is not an easy job but I do it with grace. I paved the way for those behind and beside me. You thought you won. You were so stingy with your money though you had so much more than me. I was always a giver. I was already RICHER THAN YOU. I will make more MONEY than you can ever imagine. My kids and grandchildren will have all they need all because you slept on me. Thank you for being a chapter in the story of my life. This chapter set me free and will give me financial freedom because I will tell my story, I will write books and movies, I will create programs and retreats to help others like me. I will follow God and He will show me how to maximize this experience. I will have beauty for my ashes, joy for my sorrow, I will trade poverty for abundance all because I met you and you didn't get the memo: "I am not to be played with". I hope you see my face everywhere; I hope you hear my name everywhere; I hope you never forget what has happened from 2020- 2024 and even if I never hear you say it, I hope you regret what you have done and what you have lost. Instead of pretending to be great, with me, you could have been great. Funny how life works. I asked God for an abundant life and He led me to you and though it wasn't what I thought it would be, you were my abundance in so many ways.

Dear Ex,

You Lose, I win!
- LMAO

Dear Ex,

Today was the day that I told the world (my world) who you really are and what you have done. I was so afraid and so embarrassed that this happened to me but God told me it was time. You tried to quiet me. You tried to intimidate me. You tried to break me. You even tried ignoring me. It didn't work. I am here standing in my truth and it all worked out for me. I am not surprised that it worked out for me but I am surprised you thought it wouldn't. You thought somehow you would continue as if you didn't do anything. You underestimated me and if you did that you never knew me. All I can say is "Vengeance is Mine saith the Lord" and Karma is a Bitch! Peace out dude!

- your ex-wife

Dear Ex,

Wouldn't it have been easier to be a good person instead of pretending to be a good person? You knew how much I hate lying and you challenged yourself to make my life a lie. The crazy thing is that you were never going to win because the truth is within me, the truth surrounds me, the truth is me. I am and forever will be better than you because I was real. My love was real. You lost a real one because you wanted to be a fake one. How weird.

Lakeeya Natasha

Dear Ex,

I get it now; you care more about your image and your persona than you ever cared about me. I boosted your ego and filled your cup, while you were filling my cup and poking holes in it at the same time. You had me questioning myself and going crazy out of my mind trying to understand if you were so unhappy and dissatisfied with me why didn't you leave. You didn't leave because you needed to turn the good girl into the bad guy. You needed to be able to say, "My wife left me". You needed that narrative to carry you to your next unexpected victim. She will feel sorry for you. She will promise not to hurt you the way that I did and when you begin to change on her, she will have a sense of loyalty to you because she doesn't want to cause you more hurt since you already been through so much with me. Bullshit. I am sure, if I ever get to talk to your other exes the conversation would be interesting. You better hope I don't find them and I am looking. Nothing you ever told me I believe anymore. The bare minimum truth I know is that you are a serial liar. I won't be the last one if you are not exposed. I am a good girl, better yet, I am a great woman and you couldn't handle my greatness with your weak insecure sorry ass. I would never want you back. I don't care what you tell people. I just want people to know the truth to save more victims from you and people like you. You are not even original. It's like all

Narcissists read the same damn book. You are lame. I feel sorry for you and then again, I don't. I will get the last laugh, I'm sure. You fucked over the wrong one! I don't have to be loud, yell, fight, get in your face...I just have to tell the truth. The truth sets me free and cages you.

Dear Ex,

You are not devastated or sorry, you are just mad you got caught. Bye Boy. Save it for your mother!

Dear Ex,

My business and my ass will grow now that I am not with you and you can't touch either!

Lakeeya Natasha

Dear Ex,

Today, I hosted a retreat without you and nobody missed you...not one person. You were not the leader and I think that's why your resented me so much because even on your best day, you cannot beat me on my worst day because my heart is real and really for the people not self-serving like you. You wanted people to put you on a pedestal. You got an honest woman to vouch for you but it was nothing honest about you and everyone else saw it but me. But today, I soared without you. I was so nervous when you first dropped out the retreat but each day it got closer, I gain my confidence that I could not just do it but excel at it and I did. This reassured and confirmed to me that I don't need you and never did. I wanted you and that is a huge difference. Thank you for showing me how great I can be without over compensating for your inadequacies. The art class was better than yours. The whole day was better. I am so happy. I know this is only the beginning for me. Somedays, I feel sorry you forfeited me and days like today, I barely remember you exist.

Dear Ex,

Some days I wake up and I almost forgot what happened and I am confused why I am lying in bed alone. Then it all comes rushing back in the first 30-60 seconds after I open my eyes. I take a deep breath, I read a scripture, I pray a prayer of gratitude to be alive another day and ask God for strength to be alive another day. Another deep breath and sigh as I get out of bed and make my bed-The one side I slept on. I put on a song to motivate me- sometimes gospel, sometimes meditation, sometimes rachet depends what I need to face the day. I do my stretches, take my shower, get dressed and take my little doggie on a walk. I do all of this crying or holding back my tears. I force myself to eat breakfast even if it is just a banana and I start my day. This is the 1st hour of every day. Every single day.

I don't miss our morning rituals anymore but I do remember how different my life was this time last year. I know this is for the betterment of me. I know I deserve better than you. I know I am better than you. Yet and still, I have accepted the need to grieve you and our life together every morning until I no longer need this ritual. I am getting closer to the day where my rituals won't be about getting over you because I would have forgotten you and detached from the pain you caused. I am healing and I am healed at the same time. I hope one day you begin healing for you. You will never ever be able to double back to me but

I hope you find yourself on a path of enlightenment so no other woman has to create rituals to survive you.

Dear Ex,

So, you have white savior complex, you are a lame. If you knew me at all, you would know I already have a savior and the world already knows he wasn't white. Jesus saved me a long time ago and he gave me the ability to love you even on days you were unlovable but he loved me when I didn't love Him. He gave me the ability to save myself by giving me a way of escape in all negative situations I put myself in. He gave me a way of escape from you and the prison you were trying to create for me. If you knew me you would know God doesn't allow me to fail and won't let anyone break me because no weapons formed against me prospers. You would not have ever won unless you were on my side. I didn't need a savior, I needed a lover of me, I needed a protector of me, I needed a partner, I needed a friend. You are none of those things? Cool. I moved right out your way because I will never make a man my idol when God has been so faithful to me. Go sit down somewhere because you about to see how real My God is and who I truly am.

-God's child

Dear Ex,

After every couple session I had this week, I cried because I can help other people obtain and keep healthy relationships yet I haven't found one for myself yet. I thought you were the one and I was so wrong. Now, I know why you weren't fighting for me or our relationship, because you don't have the capacity to have a healthy relationship just ones that fit who you want to pretend to be at the time. I had a moment, after you broke my heart, I thought there goes my chance of happily ever after. I recognize that I am still deserving of love because you stole something that didn't belong to you, you stole something that you were not worthy of- my heart. I am a great couples therapist because I am skilled and I know what it takes to be a great partner. I was a great partner to you. I will be a great partner when a real man comes along. Thank you for showing your true colors sooner than later.

Dear Ex,

Today was supposed to be our anniversary. Instead, I had people calling

and texting me all day and night checking on me. Everyone expected me to be wallowing in sadness. I am sad but I am not missing you. I am sad that I loved you so much and it wasn't real. How can my true love be a complete lie? So, I guess you told the truth when you said you never loved anyone before because you are incapable of love. That saddens me. It saddens me to know that me loving you wasn't enough for you to experience love. I am sad for you. I will love again; I am sure of it because God would not make my greatest love a fake. I will take my time. I will enjoy being single and free. I will use what you taught me to weed out other narcissists and toxic lovers. I will use our experiences together to make new experiences with people that appreciate

me. I will use my sexual awakening to enjoy all forms of pleasure. The four years with you wasn't all a loss. I hate you for what you have done but I release you in love so when I am ready your dead weight will no longer be my anchor. I will soar again. I will love and be loved again. Next time it will be for real. Happy Anniversary!

Lakeeya Natasha

Dear Ex,

I wanted to thank you because you created so many growth opportunities for me. Now, do I understand that it was not your intention to grow me but to use me. I am learning so much about narcissistic abuse and I am learning so much about myself. I know the level of neglect I experienced in previous relationships and thirst for passion, love, lust, adventure made me extremely vulnerable for your love bombing. It felt so good to me to have someone pursuing me so strongly and so quickly yet I didn't trust my instinct. I was so fresh from separation even though it was 2 years in the making and the divorce was inevitable, I was not healed enough to be in any serious relationship. I told you in the first few dates that I was not looking to be in a relationship until after my divorce was final. You were insistent that I didn't need to be alone while I was going through the process.

The person I am today would have used that as a signal to run the other way. I never had a man apply so much pressure and it was flattering and so needed for my self-esteem after being divorced twice. Every early concern I had was matched with comments from you and others that I was "self-sabotaging". I was told my fear and apprehension was because I have never fell so intensely for someone that felt the same way back. I know now that it was my spirit telling me to slow down and observe him. Is he a good guy or is he using your relationship to look good? Does he have the same morals and values? Are you trying to make him a better person? Were you trying to elevate him to your level? Once I got to know you and seen how you lived, I instantly made you my project like I did with every other man. I began cleaning and remodeling your house and turned it into a functional home because it was dirty and uninhabitable. You living that way was evidence enough that we didn't value the same things. I bought your clothes for when we went on vacation because you definitely didn't match my swag. You didn't and still don't care about your appearance or cleanliness. Your kids had no structure, discipline, or motivation because you didn't instill that or promote that in them because you didn't have that instilled in you. You grew up so privileged, without any accountability, so you are a very selfish, spoiled, lazy, entitled man. You were the epitome of white privilege but you wore the mask of a caring man, social worker with black kids he rescued from their "crazy mom".

In hindsight, I wish I talked to her alone and really asked her what happened with your relationship because I'll bet you did the same to her as you did to me but she wasn't equipped to take you on so she lost and her kids lost being with you. You fooled everyone just like you fooled me. However; you taught me to love myself. You taught me that I am a generous, kind, loving person. You taught me that I am a mirror and I am light. I am something you can never be, Real. You taught me that I had the ability to honor my vows, submit to my husband, and commit to building a life with a new family. You taught me I already had everything I needed inside me. You taught me that right outside my comfort zone, I would find new friends, new music, new experiences that I will be forever grateful for. You taught me that love is not enough to save a lost soul unless they want to be saved. You taught me that my faith is too important to compromise.

I would have never known who I really was until I met a demon like you, who was so scared of me finding out who I was that you tried to disable me. You tried everything to degrade and belittle me and nothing worked. I left you. You had the house, the money, the land, the white privilege and I LEFT YOU- How pathetic do you feel? I left you to live in your filth and I moved to a peaceful fresh clean start. I am better without you and I am better because of you. I cannot wait until the day I lose your last name. It is worthless to me because I married a ghost- a person that never existed.

I loved a lie. I am working on forgiving myself. I know it was not my fault but I should have taken heed of the signs. As I heal, date, and love again- I will use this experience to guide me, to remind me that my intuitive spirit is connected to God's plan for my life and I will trust my gut and leave first time I notice inconsistencies. I will run away from any and all love bombing behaviors and I will exit stage left if a man doesn't share my core morals and values. I will now consider our relationship, a situationship that became a four-year long bootcamp. Your bootcamp prepared me and set me free- funny that it is the opposite of your mission. I graduated with honors. I know you wanted a sex maid; you literally could have bought one of those and saved me and my kids a lot of

tears. You are pond scum and I am so glad you dropped your mask when you did. Thank you.

-Lesson Learned

Dear Ex,

I am so grateful God gave me a way of escape and I pray one day you find true healing and repentance. I truly hope God saves you or takes you so no one has to endure what you have done to me.

Praying for you,

Lakeeya

Lakeeya Natasha

Dear Ex,

I am actually surprised how much I don't miss you. I recognize that I had to recalibrate my nervous system from all the egg shell walking I had to do to make it work with you once I realized how little stress management skills you had. I cared about you so much. I made every excuse I could for you and bent so much to help you adjust to our new life. I bent so much I almost broke so leaving you was the only thing for me to do to stay intact once you made it clear that you had no desire to change. I found peace being away from you and am only triggered when thinking

about having to interact with you. This is why I know I will never miss you. You are an unsafe person to me, actually the most unsafe because you pretended to be safe until I dropped all my guards then pounced like a hunter to its prey. I am glad I escaped. I reconciled that our love wasn't real.

I don't grieve you. I grieve what you have done. I grieve that any new relationship I have will be scrutinized my me and by people who love me. I grieve that fact I will struggle with dating after multiple failed relationships. I grieve the idea of falling in love, for any relationship I will find myself in will take a lot of work just to feel safe. It is unfair to the next person, who had nothing to do with my scars. The idea that this 4-year relationship stole my fairy tale ending is sometimes unbearable but I am grateful for all I learned about myself and my capacity to love myself and others.

I don't miss you but I wonder about you from time to time, hoping my true love for you planted a seed in your heart where remorse can grow. I want you to heal but not for me. Your healing will prevent you from hurting another person like you hurt me. I know, most likely, you won't change or even feel like you have to. You have no need to change when people are still hell bent to only seeing the mask you wear. Without accountability and awareness, growth can't occur. All I can do is settle into my new life, trust the process, and be open to love again once it presents itself. This process is exhausting. The heaviness only sits with the victim never the perpetrator- that's how I know who I am and who you are in this scenario. I welcome the day when I never think of you again and this time of my life.

-Over it

Lakeeya Natasha

Dear Ex,

I went through all of the emotions for sure. I am still hurt by all you have done. Some things I probably will never share with anyone because it was truly horrific and nasty (you know what I am talking about) but if I didn't have this relationship I would not have met

many new friends and colleagues I have, I would not have met my bonus babies, I would not have learned so much about myself and how deep I can love someone. If not for you, I would not have known how much I could tolerate and how resilient I am. I thought I fell in love with you but you were just pretending to be like me. When your mask came off, you freed me. I can move in peace and gratitude. I am forever changed from this experience in some very sad and traumatic ways and some really powerful ways. The only thing I regret is marrying you because I could have gotten the same lesson as your girlfriend and moved on to find my husband but now, I am 3 times divorced and not sure if anyone will take a chance on marrying me or would I even want to. I wish you healing. I hope one day you find peace within yourself to not hurt someone trying to love you.

- Keeya

Dear Ex,

I want to thank you truly and completely. The love you gave and the pain you exchanged it for were both needed gifts, that allowed me to see myself truly, for the first time in my life. Our time together changed my life forever and even though I thought it was for forever, I do understand why it could not be. You were my greatest love and greatest lesson. Such deep pain comes from knowing I actually surrendered to love and gave it my very best effort. I opened my heart and began to believe that I deserved the life I always imagined. I took a leap of faith and the first time in my life I felt loved. I appreciated every moment of it. Whether it was even real, some parts real, or all a game you played, I may never know. I do know what I felt and the depth of what I had to offer. The feeling filled me and gave me the ability to fill others. You gave so many people hope of true love the second or third time around. I thank you for revealing yourself, as it allowed me to put who I know I am to the test. If I could walk away from what I thought was true love when it shows itself as cruel and relentless- I can walk into any new situation, opportunity or relationship with the same boldness. For I realized that you were my mirror. The mask you wore was Me and when I fell in love with you, I really fell in love with myself. Maybe, it was that part, that made you resent me but I no longer will ruminate on such things. It is over. We both know that. I don't know if there is a better version of yourself awaiting. I don't know if you even want to change. What I do know is I am better for it. I am better from all of it, even the parts too dark for me to share with anyone. Those twisted moments will be kept safe within my soul where forgiveness and grace with cover them. I will no longer feel bad for trying to be whatever my husband wanted. I am grateful I had the desire to grow with someone and heal for someone. Thank you for being my inspiration. I realized that we were "until death do us part" because your treachery killed the last of naive, people pleasing, insecure Lakeeya. She is gone. What will rise from her ashes, I am curious to find out. I take comfort that you will never know her. Goodbye, my love. I release you with gratitude. I hope you find peace in your actions. I have found peace in mine.

- Your 2nd Ex Wife

Dear Ex,

There is so many beautiful remnants of you in my life. You added so much value to me and for that I will always hold gratitude for the time we shared. However, you hurt me deeper than any person I ever encountered. You broke me, in a way, I never knew I could break. You shattered my confidence in love. For those reasons, I struggle to forgive you. I pray for you every time that pain visits me because I need to forgive you for me. Forgiving you will allow me to be available for love again and I do want to experience love, real love one day. The love I gave you was real and I pray it planted in your heart and will help you grow into the man I thought you were. The love I gave you is the same love I deserve so I will give it to myself. I will keep working on forgiving you so when my person does come, he will not live in your shadow but in my light.

- trying to forgive

Lakeeya Natasha

Dear Ex,

I have to take responsibility for hurting my own feelings. Throughout the early stages of the relationship and even in our friendship before the intimacy, you shown me time and time again who you really are and even said things that were a foreshadowing for the heartache to come. Your mixed approach of push and pull, I accepted, as some sort of challenge to prove my worthiness, while you were grooming me to need your constant validation. You told me love was conditional and you have never loved anyone before. What a RED FLAG yet you shown me what felt like love so I just thought I was different and I was the one you were waiting for. There were so many examples of this yet I leaned into your potential and not who you were. You were cruel and unkind but I broke my own heart.

I am not the same girl you first met and we both knew it in 2023. I did change and you were exactly who you are always going to be - a manipulative covert victim narcissist with catastrophic mother wounds. You prey on women whose brokenness wants to save you. You are right to leave me because that was the only way I would have left you. Thank-you for showing me how to love myself and I hope one day you get to experience self-love too.

- Accepting and Surrendering

Dear Ex,

You know what...I been sulking for months over a man that never existed. I missed the man you never were but only pretended to me. I will feel sorry for any woman that has to deal with you moving forward and who dealt with you in the past. You are trainwreck pretending to be a first-class flight. It is laughable how you go through the world giving advice to people who you could never measure up against. You are a clown for sure! I made you look good for 3.5 years and so good you started to believe you are better off without me. Foolish. I am better off without you, most definitely. There are so many more things I would not miss about you than I miss. On today, I can't honestly say I miss nothing because I met a man that rocks my socks in bed, that makes my legs shake, and I soaked the bed with him. What else did you offer me but some great orgasms???

Nothing.

I won't miss the anxiety you caused me.

I won't miss your lack of cleanliness and organization.

I won't miss cleaning up after you.

I won't miss your lack of motivation and your constant complaining on how bad your life is as a man of privilege.

I won't miss your ugly cargo pants and dingy t-shirts.

I won't miss your downward spirals every time any obstacle came your way.

I won't miss your lack of faith and inability to have hope for tomorrow.

I won't miss your constant drinking and beer cans and empty liquor bottles you would not clear off the table.

I won't miss your nasty habits.

I won't miss your selfishness.

I won't miss your cheapness when it comes to things I wanted and how you spent money on stupid things you wanted all the time.

I won't miss the acts you put on in front of my friends and family.

I won't miss your lack of leadership.

I won't miss your racist comments.

I won't miss your need to be coddled.

I won't miss your anger.

I won't miss your ability to let me do all the work and you stand beside me like we did it as a team.

I won't miss you controlling when and how I could go to the bathroom.

I won't miss your lack of personal hygiene.

I won't miss having to pick out your clothes if we go out.

I won't miss your constant lying and gaslighting.

I won't miss the way you snored while I cried myself to sleep.

I won't miss how you ran over to your mommy every time you couldn't cope.

I won't miss your lack of communication.

I won't miss how you talk about people then hug them.

I absolutely will not miss you.

I grieve only for the years I thought I knew you and the marriage you robbed me of. You are a horrible person and I hope you see me and every woman you hurt every time you look in the mirror. I would not have divorced you. I wanted you to get help and change. So, thank you for showing me who you really are, your inability to change, and definitely for divorcing me.

-Your ex-wife

Dear Ex,

One day, I will wake up next to another man and I won't be thinking of you. One day, someone will make me moan and call out their name. One day, I will crave the touch of someone other than you. One day, you will be irrelevant. One day, another man will stumble across an

amazing woman that healed, whole, super sexy, smart, driven, nurturing, independent yet submissive, playful, sensual, and hyper sexual and he will snatch her up and think to himself her ex must have been crazy to let this Queen go. One Day...

Dear Ex,

What did you think was going to happen?!?! You did a woman of God wrong; how do you expect to have a good life after that. You returned the gift the Universe gave you so say Hello to Karma...

Dear Ex,

I loved you deeply and I forgive you. I truly wish you well and thank you for the journey and the lesson. This burden has released itself. I am free now.

-Lakeeya Natasha

bonus letters to my younger self, future self, and current self

Dear Baby Girl,

Whatever you desire is available to you. If you haven't seen it yet doesn't mean that it doesn't exist. If you haven't seen it yet but desire it just know either you are not ready for it or it is being readied for you. God will give you the desires of your heart but not at the detriment of your soul. Your soul work will take you what feels like several lifetimes. You will experience many losing seasons yet you will never lose. Your anxiety will tell you to settle, to work harder, to try to be more loveable, to shrink back, to be quiet, to be loud, to compromise your morals. Your trauma will tell you that you are broken, over-rated, unworthy, too little and too much. This is not true. This is not your truth. A deep Knowing within you, will not allow you to succumb to these thoughts.

You know this and will know this truth on your darkest days- You are Magic. You are Light. You are a Mirror. You are an ever-evolving butterfly. You are a Thunderstorm and You are a shelter from the rain. I want you to quiet your mind so that you can hear only the truth- you were born with a value that cannot be tainted or tarnished. You were worthy from the beginning of time. Nothing you can do can diminish your worth or dim your light. No crime or wrongdoing done against your mind or body can devalue you. Nope, not even that. You were brought to the earth for such a time as this because you are needed here. Your spirit is needed here. Your gifts and talents will be your guide. The natural story of your birth may seem unfortunate and haphazard but best believe it was a miracle. You are a miracle. You will see and perform many miracles in your many lifetimes. Keep your eyes open for them.

Your mission will be to Love and to be Loved. You will start with others and grow weary. You will try to give all your love away with the thought that someone else's love for you would replenish it. You will just hover close to empty. Your love must start and end with you. This and only this will allow you to love others so dynamically. You are a healer and this is how you will heal others. Your superpower is Love and you are your own supply because God is within you. Love yourself so deeply, completely, truly, unapologetically and you will shift atmospheres. Your love will change time and space. Your love will heal the Broken-hearted. Your love will motivate the lost. Your love will cause a revolution because your Love will give people permission to Love Themselves too.

You are a hopeful romantic and you must never give up on love. You will love many times and no matter how hard it gets your heart will not stop loving. To your own surprise, you will remain open for love because you are love. Your journey will not be easy baby girl. There will be days that will feel unbearable. The grief that awaits you on this journey is indescribable and for that I wish I could protect you from most it. The grief is the platform you must stand boldly. For who will marvel at a butterfly in a garden, a few, because it is expected to be there yet a butterfly in a desert has everyone's attention. It should not be able to survive its conditions but there it is. Some will watch to see if the wings will burn. Some will watch, in awe, as it seemingly floats above its dusty environment. No matter why they are looking, they are all looking and as they look they will have no choice to be transformed as well. That's magic. You should not be able to survive the conditions you will be sent to but you will. You will thrive. It will be okay even when it is not okay. I promise.

Every mistake you will ever make is already forgiven by God and by me so don't be afraid to make them. Mistakes make you human- rising above your mistakes makes you supernatural. I send you only compassion and a fresh wind for your journey to me. Your desires await you baby girl. Your tribe awaits you baby girl. Your vision awaits you baby girl. Your truest love awaits you baby girl. Remember, you are purpose and you are purposed.

Sincerely,

Your future Self

Lakeeya Natasha

To Keeya 2024,

Deep breaths girl. You have been through the ringer. Your entire life is a testament that what doesn't kill you makes you stronger. I know you are tired of being strong, weary of your resilience but that is who you are. You are so real; it is almost unbelievable. From a shy girl who barely wanted people to notice her to a phenomenal woman owning her fierceness, her brilliance, her sensuality, her sexuality. You had every excuse to shrink back this year but you didn't. You forged ahead and began owning your status as Big Pressure. You doubled down on your healing journey and practiced what you preached. You had no idea what was in store for you but everything in your life prepared you to walk into this new and unexpected season with such poise, grace, and attitude. BRAVERY IS AN UNDERSTATEMENT.

You mean what you say and say what you mean which is the first time since you were a little girl whose voice was stifled when it became inconvenient. I am loving self-love on you. I am excited for what is next but I am content where you are right now. You decided to give yourself permission to feel all the feelings and honor them- that is so brave in a world that finds the truth bothersome. You threw away the rule book and enjoying your desires and experiences. You have fewer yet stronger friendships. You have the respect and support of your children and family. You have new male prospects. You have

DearEx,

endless ways to improve your finances and move closer to the freedom you always wanted. You are the beauty and you are the beast. You don't need a man to save you because you saved yourself. Life is bright for you. Do not get discouraged in the initial hustle back to your baseline, it will all be fruitful in the end. Your credit and bank account will be back soon enough. You will be restored and go higher than ever before. God always show up for you. God is always ready to blow your mind so just keep doing what you are doing and you will see sooner than you think ALL THINGS WORK OUT FOR YOUR GOOD!

-Me

Dear Future Self,

I don't know who you are yet but I am already so dam proud of you. I see you Queen. Living and Thriving, Crying and Laughing, Giving encouragement and Receiving support, Making money and Blessing others. I can't wait to hear how you made it over. I love you...see you soon Queen!

How To Survive a Breakup

Recovering from a breakup can be challenging, but with time and self-care, it becomes easier. Here are some steps to help you heal:

1. Allow Grief to Visit You: It's okay to feel sad, angry, or confused. Give yourself permission to process these emotions without rushing.

2. Lean on Support: Reach out to friends, family, or a therapist. Talking about your feelings can provide relief and perspective. You don't have to share everything with everybody but find your tribe that you can be authentic and vulnerable with.

3. Focus on Self-Care: Prioritize your physical and emotional health. Exercise, eat well, and get enough rest. Engage in activities that bring you joy and relaxation. Say no to people, places, and things that drain the little energy you have outside of your obligations i.e. Work, school, raising children

4. Avoid Rebound Decisions: Resist the urge to jump into a new serious relationship or make impulsive choices. Take time to rediscover yourself. *Casual Dating can be a fun and healthy distraction if done right. *

5. Reflect on the Relationship: Once emotions settle, reflect on what you learned from the experience and how it can help you grow.

6. Set Boundaries: If staying in touch with your ex hinders your healing, consider setting boundaries, like limiting or cutting off contact temporarily.

7. Rediscover Hobbies: Reconnect with activities or interests you might have neglected during the relationship. They can help you regain a sense of identity. Try new activities as you are also a changed person and might enjoy something different.

8. Set New Goals: Focus on personal growth and set new goals, whether related to career, health, or creative pursuits. This is where your glow up is born!

9. Give Yourself Time: Healing is a gradual process. Be patient with yourself and trust that with time, things will get better.

10. Refrain Avoiding your Feelings: Numbing out through alcohol, drugs, sex, or excessive working will just make the pain worse and last longer. I know it is hard but feel it without masking as much as possible and get professional help if you are already struggling with any of these.

11. DANCE YOUR PAIN AWAY!!!! Movement releases the trauma energy in your body so put on your music- Dance & Release

About the Author

Lakeeya Natasha is a licensed clinical social worker, therapist, motivational speaker, author, and wellness coach. Lakeeya is a mother of three amazing individuals. She is a daughter, sister, auntie, and friend. Lakeeya is a survivor of childhood trauma, domestic violence, and three failed marriages. Lakeeya has her Master's Degree in Social Work from Temple University. After years of working in various mental health settings, she launched her own private practice in 2018. Transitions4Life, LLC offers mobile and telehealth to busy professionals. Through Transitions4Life LLC, Lakeeya assists individuals, families, couples, and corporate groups in becoming more aware of specific patterns that are keeping them stuck and preventing them from moving forward. She is an advocate in normalizing therapy for wounded healers. In 2020, Transitions4Life LLC added crisis and pandemic support to the list of services provided and has already serviced many companies in the tristate area. She provides the tools and strategies that people need to overcome their obstacles to live their best life and find their defined freedom despite uncertain times. As she was building her private practice, she knew she wanted to help new therapists and future entrepreneurs, so she wrote a series of clinical booklets; *Progress Notes Made Simple, Treatment Plans Made Simple, and The Goal Chasers Guide to Clinical Practice.* In 2022, she created OTOTM (One Trip Over the Moon, LLC) coaching and consulting practice, where she addresses professional burnout, selfcare, and desire for meaningful connections in this post-Covid world.

Despite all her accomplishments, degrees, and awards...her greatest mission was to heal her own inner child and show that girl love. This book is to honor that little girl with the big feelings with nowhere to put them without consequence. Lakeeya Natasha wanted to show everyone that she was just a girl who desired love yet instead gain another lesson. She wanted to show that helpers oftentimes find themselves needing help. Additionally; Lakeeya wanted to encourage more people to use writing as a coping strategy.

For more information about Transitions4Life please contact askkeeya@gmail.com or go to www.transitions4life.com

For more information about OTOTM please contact onetripoverthemoon@gmail.com or go to www.onetripretreats.com

Made in the USA
Columbia, SC
13 January 2025

3ecaf409-b38a-4a3a-8c14-4760619c94f8R01